I0786034

The INFJ Anthology

A collection of poems, prose and quotations from the rarest personality type

Copyright © 2017 Peta Maria Slaney

All rights reserved. This book or any portion thereof may not be reproduced or used in any manner whatsoever without the express written permission of the author except for the use of brief quotations in a book review.

First Printing, 2017

This edition, 2018

ISBN 978-1721921935

For E, L & V. Always and Forever.

Table of Contents

Foreword by Julia McGuinness

Within these pages is an unusual gathering: poetry, prose and quotations from representatives of the world's rarest personality type: We INFJs are reputed to comprise around just 1% of the population amongst the 16 types posited by the Myers-Briggs® Personality Type Model.

Sometimes collectively referred to as 'an empathy of INFJs,' we offer words reflecting themes appropriate to this personality type's concerns with relationships and authenticity; self and soul; connection and completion; life and death; the inner life and the stuff of dreams and imagination.

The understated outer presentation of the often soft-spoken INFJ belies a kaleidoscopic inner world of complexity, colour and adventure. So the depth of feeling, intensity of experience and creative shifts of perspectives revealed by my fellow INFJs in this anthology hold no astonishment for me.

Interspersed with contemporary poems are words of writers and thinkers past, whose lives and writing suggest a strong identification with the INFJ Personality Type.

Amongst them, Dostoevsky and Hawthorne have become new soulmates, as I've found myself murmuring a quiet 'yes' to their insights.

It has been observed of this type that, 'we mean every word.' This makes the focus and precision of poetry a particularly INFJ-friendly medium. INFJS are lovers of symbol and seekers of connection, drawn to the potential of images to express what is on their inmost hearts. The poetic form also sits well with our preference for creating outer order and shape.

Poetry contains and distills emotion, experience and insight. Coleridge's definition of it as 'the best words in the best order,' resonates with INFJs who strive for the best - hopefully perfect - words to bring into being those things for which there are not yet words. Such catching and communicating of the inexpressible is a challenge INFJs are up for, typically turning to metaphor, image and paradox as their means of meeting it.

This anthology reflects the concerns of the INFJ's world. Love is foremost among them. The introvert's focus is on one-to-one relationships - the transformational impact of 'the meeting of two personalities' commented on by Jung and expressed in Anita's image of twin rocks smoothed into beached pebbles,' emptying our souls to one another.'

INFJs treasure such intimacy, but it is risky territory for this naturally private type. It may be embraced in an intense intuitive response, as with Bronte's *Jane Eyre*, or approached more tentatively, as in Paul Rossener's *She*.

An idealising tendency can make the INFJs' experience of the envisioned relationship short-lived. Acutely attuned to another's emotions, INFJs hurt deeply when love goes awry, evident in Peta Maria Slaney's *Torn Asunder,* and her exploring of the courage needed in *Learning to Love Again.*

The heartfelt emotion of loss - of relationship, of health, a loved one's presence, drives the INFJ to seek words, not just to salve the pain, but also as a quest for understanding and underlying meaning that will restore equilibrium and hope.

INFJs have a natural future-orientation; several poems illustrate the seeking of new possibilities in a sweeping rise from the 'ashes' to 'high skies' of Slaney's *Introspection Part*

II. Though perhaps only an INFJ anthology would choose as its final line a determination to 'bear alone the weary strife.'

INFJs see the outer world through an imaginative inner lens, as in the child's view of the sky in Rossener's *Up*. In tough times, however, everyday life can become a 'soul assault' that intrudes on deeper matters, as Anita observes. It may also be a troublesome place of sensory excess for the INFJ under stress. Kaisa Hammeren takes a wry look at this contrariness as an INFJ moment of clear insight into life gives way to the compulsive - but clandestine - consumption of a stash of Snickers bars.

Hammeren is also aware of the paradoxical nature of writing for INFJs. Drawn so strongly towards words as a bridge to the outer world from the complexities of their inner one, INFJs still feel their best words may fall short of conveying all they would wish - an issue expressed in *Lost in Translation*

We hope, nevertheless, that more has been found than lost in the poetry that follows, and that our offering will excite and inspire those of all personality types, fostering a deeper

connection between us. And if you feel a need for your own voice to be heard more loud and clear, we invite other types to follow with their own anthologies where INFJs have - in all modesty of course - quietly gone before.

Julia McGuinness

Preface by Peta Maria Slaney

The inspiration for this collection comes from the many INFJ blogs and forum posts discussing our preference for writing over making small talk. I have heard it said many times that INFJs make wonderful writers and poets; and that some of our most famous and beloved authors were in fact INFJs.

This led me down the rabbit hole of researching classic INFJ writers; those who had been typed posthumously and whose emotions resonated so strongly with us. After a while, I noticed that the same names would come up again and again. It was just such a shame that their works had not been collated and put together. I decided to put together a small collection for my own personal perusal, but after speaking to some of my closest friends and a few online enquiries, the idea of the INFJ Anthology was born.

This edition includes work from classical poets and writers, as well as submissions from INFJs all around the world. As the poems started to arrive, I would fill with emotion as their thoughts resonated with me; the depth of feeling and range of experiences were joyous to discover.

Whilst every effort has been made to obtain copyrights of all poems, most of those from our classical poets are in the public domain.

I hope that reading through this collection brings you joy and peace, and that you are swept along through our writers' experiences and emotions. The anthology has been split into three sections, so you can either work your way through in order, or dip and dive as the mood takes you.

Please enjoy.

Peta Maria Slaney

Section One

Love & Friendship

From Jane Eyre by Charlotte Bronte

"I have for the first time found what I can truly love–I have found you. You are my sympathy–my better self–my good angel–I am bound to you with a strong attachment. I think you good, gifted, lovely: a fervent, a solemn passion is conceived in my heart; it leans to you, draws you to my centre and spring of life, wrap my existence about you–and, kindling in pure, powerful flame, fuses you and me in one."

From White Nights by Fyodor Dostoyevsky

"I am a dreamer. I know so little of real life that I just can't help re-living such moments as these in my dreams, for such moments are something I have very rarely experienced. I am going to dream about you the whole night, the whole week, the whole year. I feel I know you so well that I couldn't have known you better if we'd been friends for twenty years. You won't fail me, will you? Only two minutes, and you've made me happy forever. Yes, happy. Who knows, perhaps you've reconciled me with myself, resolved all my doubts.

When I woke up it seemed to me that some snatch of a tune I had known for a long time, I had heard somewhere before but had forgotten, a melody of great sweetness, was coming back to me now. It seemed to me that it had been trying to emerge from my soul all my life, and only now-

If and when you fall in love, may you be happy with her. I don't need to wish her anything, for she'll be happy with you. May your sky always be clear, may your dear smile always be bright and happy, and may you be for ever blessed for that moment of bliss and happiness which you gave to another lonely and grateful heart. Isn't such a moment sufficient for the whole of one's life?"

She by Paul Rossener

I didn't enjoy the first time

We went out together

Her arm close to mine as

We squeezed under

My umbrella

I tried to make sense of all things

My brain was overheating

Her words were disappearing as

I did

My best to make a mental recording of

Her that day

Her height almost near mine

Her voice inflecting whenever

She found a new thing to say

She had a lot to say

I had a lot to hear

We had a lot to share

We shared from 10:31 to 11:29

Our fleeting time and

My heart was racing but

I kept
My composure, while
She kept being
Her charming self

She waved goodbye and
I went on my way and that's the time that
I suddenly was able to process all the things that had
happened during that day

I sat down, chills crawled from
My neck down
My eyes got watery because
I didn't enjoy the first time
We went out together until
I stopped
My mental recording. Hit rewind and
I played it again.

She was lovely that day

By C. G. Jung

"The meeting of two personalities is like the contact of two chemical substances: if there is any reaction, both are transformed."

Next Time by Anita Traynor

I've been thinking, on and off, about seeing you again.
How would it be, next time?
Too shy to acknowledge your honesty? too ashamed to
see the truth?
Too scared to make our encounter count?

More excuses, absolute control, a veil of platitudes and
politeness
Exaggerating the distance between us.

The curse of heart rules head but head holds heart in
shackles,
Excess strangled;

Regrets? Too late. Excuses? Too many.
But maybe. In another lifetime.

"…if a man can be properly said to love something, it must be clear that he feels affection for it as a whole, and does not love part of it to the exclusion of the rest."

My Mother's Emerald Ring by Julia McGuinness

Circled a finger on hands that tended me;

deft and gemmed with green stone,

bringer of healing and calm; exotic

as Creme de Menthe or depths marine.

Ring set with a 9 by 6mm emerald

exquisite as a baby's fingernail;

Father's gift for the gift of me,

Birthstone for my month of May

and green years of bare feet

on dewed grass; lime-tanged sweets

in sticky hoards; her ring's flash

as she made me a dress to match.

Her hands wrinkled, mind slowed

to ringless days in the Care Home.

I placed her emerald safe in a box,

dulled to a pebble of memory.

Her hands grown cold as stone

still I kept her ring in the dark;

carried it close as a secret

till I could gaze on it again

and see more clear and deep

a heart gardened with light,

pure-bodied green flawed

in patient containing of other.

I stroke its grazed edge,

put emerald on my finger;

brush my lips across its face;

cushion it with a kiss.

"All my heart is yours, sir: it belongs to you; and with you it would remain, were fate to exile the rest of me from your presence forever."

Love is by Peta Maria Slaney

Love is what keeps me sane.

Love is what keeps me humble.

Love is what helps me move forward when everything seems too much.

Love is the North Star, unwavering, unchanging.

Love is always there to guide me.

Love makes me so much more than I am.

Love is the path that leads through adversity and onwards to hope and happiness.

Love is everything.

"According to Greek mythology, humans were originally created with four arms, four legs and a head with two faces. Fearing their power, Zeus split them into two separate parts, condemning them to spend their lives in search of their other halves."

I Chose You by Anna Tisna

I chose you

You, who I trusted

You, who I wanted to be with

I was foolish too

For it couldn't have lasted

Years have passed

Since my last doorslam

But the pain lasted

Now my world is bland

I wish I did it differently

So I wouldn't ache painfully

But deep inside I know clearly

That it wouldn't have turned out differently

Welcome and Farewell by Goethe

My heart was beating, swiftly to horse!

Faster even than thought it was done.

Already evening cradled earth's course,

And night hung over the mountain cone:

Already the misty oak-tree stood,

A vast giant, towering upwards there,

Where from out the shadowy wood

A hundred dark eyes seemed to stare.

From a bank of cloud the Moon gazed,

Sadly out of the mist about her,

The winds beat soft wings, and strayed

Around my terror-stricken ears:

The night begot a thousand monsters,

But my spirit was joyful, lively:

Deep inside my veins what fire!

Deep inside my heart what heat!

I saw you, and full measure of bliss

Flowed to me from your sweet eyes:

I drew for you my every breath,

My heart was wholly on your side.

Springtime's rose-red glow, it shone

All about your lovely face, lit

Tenderly for me – dear God!

I had hoped, but not deserved it!

But ah, already at morning light

My heart was crushed in parting:

In your kisses what delight!

In your eyes what suffering!

I went, you stood, looked from above,

And saw me go with tearful gaze:

And yet what joy to be loved!

Dear God, to love what happiness!

Friends At The Beach by Anita Traynor

We are two rough edged rocks

Hewn from the shadows

We are each other's sea

Waves cajoling craggy corners into curves

Sometimes splashing splintered shards into smoothness

Until we lie still side by side on the beach

Now two rounded pebbles

Staring upward

Raw with cold.

Thoughts and feelings shoot high to

Puncture the blackness with

Stars which leak healing tears.

Moon tugs tides

Where minds won't dare to peek

Teasing and tearing hearts.

When the spinning world stops still

And we have emptied our souls each to the other

The horizon will tilt a little and

A lone gull will hug another sunrise

From The Scarlet Letter by Nathaniel Hawthorne

"It is a curious subject of observation and inquiry, whether hatred and love be not the same thing at bottom. Each, in its utmost development, supposes a high degree of intimacy and heart-knowledge; each renders one individual dependent for the food of his affections and spiritual life upon another; each leaves the passionate lover, or the no less passionate hater, forlorn and desolate by the withdrawal of his object."

From Vita Nuova by Dante Alighieri

"In that book which is my memory,

On the first page of the chapter that is the day when I first met you,

Appear the words, 'Here begins a new life'."

Beyond The Line by Julia McGuinness

I was your kept woman,

a good enough arrangement.

You championed my colours on the field.

I rested in the tent, ready

to tend tattered flesh,

calm pacing pride.

You were my hero, you said it yourself,

and, to be fair, you were generous with your spoils -

Our spoils, you said.

Yet what glowed gold in the firelight

turned hollow tin by grey dawn.

Crackling petals dropped from faded garlands.

I grew weary of sweeping them up.

For there was never an end to this war;

no final victory; no talk of truce.

When your eyes faced mine,

I saw only my image,

your deeper gaze aflame with

fantasies of the next campaign.

I kept my counsel, chose my time

to push past you on the front line.

Your armour's cold shoulder made me shudder,

but my skin warmed in the sun;

my linen dress billowed in the breeze

across No Man's Land;

grass oozed green under my naked feet.

I looked back at you, tiny creature;

Stone-still with rage, your sword slipping your grip.

All you knew was fighting,

claimed you were my servant;

let me believe you were my master.

I pressed on,

finding my footing across the bright field.

Our foe disarmed by my unshielded smile —

no war-shrieks; no clang of metal —

the warm hands of a shy stranger

welcomed me into a waiting tent.

In the clear-eyed gaze of this new alliance,

we finally knew our selves.

"Because misery, and degradation, and death, and nothing that God or Satan could inflict would have parted us, you, of your own will did it. I have no broken your heart - you have broken it; and in breaking it, you have broken mine. So much the worse for me that I am strong."

It's scary. Dipping your toes in the water,

Knowing that it could all go horribly wrong.

It's exciting. Reawakening all those emotions that

Had been shut away and locked up.

It's terrifying. Going into it with your eyes wide open,

Fully aware of how much you have to lose.

It's empowering. Choosing to love despite the past.

Surrendering, trusting, growing, allowing yourself to be

loved.

"What is hell? I maintain that it is the suffering of being
unable to love."

"Love is born into every human being; it calls back the halves of our original nature together; it tries to make one out of two and heal the wound of human nature."

Retrospective by Julia McGuinness

Framed by station platforms:

Blue Monday in Manchester.

Damp lingers on pavements

like undried paint.

The Gallery in waiting

holds hush and footfall's echo.

We enter its sanctuary

at the borders of ordinary time.

We drift through rooms windowed

with 'Manchester's Monet':

lime-lit poise of *The Picnic;*

gauzy haze of *The Blue Valley.*

He painted as, not what, he saw.

'Look,' you say, 'how daubs

of purple catch the ultra-violet' -

light in which we have our being.

We press into memory's palette,

loosen colours of three decades.

Your voice, soft walnut-brown,

recalls reluctance to read aloud.

I bring new-mint green as 'Ma'am.'

The air is oiled by grace.

Broken colour blends gold

as bracken in *Evening Shadows.*

Lunch - a gallery of salads,

collaged on white-primed plates:

olive, beetroot, butternut.

Impasto talk textures the hours

with frail mothers, fatherhood,

coffee shop bliss and Radio 4.

New layers cream old into relief;

We cross-hatch anecdotes over cake.

On the homeward train

distance gifts definition.

A canvas, more than restored,

settling in interior space.

I see the carriage window

flat-imaged with faces.

Twilight sky shimmers.

Purple-flecked.

This poem arose from a re-union with one of my first English A-Level students, after over 30 years. I taught him at High Wycombe's Royal Grammar School, where female teachers were always addressed as 'Ma'am.

"I think... if it is true that

there are as many minds as there

are heads, then there are as many

kinds of love as there are hearts."

From The Scarlet Letter by Nathaniel Hawthorne

"Love, whether newly born or aroused from a deathlike slumber, must always create sunshine, filling the heart so full of radiance, that it overflows upon the outward world."

From Wuthering Heights by Emily Bronte

"He's more myself than I am. Whatever our souls are made of, his and mine are the same. If all else perished, and he remained, I should still continue to be; and if all else remained, and he were annihilated, the universe would turn to a mighty stranger."

"He's more myself than I am. Whatever our souls are

New Love, New Life by Goethe

Heart, my heart, what can it mean?

What could trouble you so?

What a strange new life, it seems!

You, I no longer know.

Everything you loved is done,

Everything that grieved you,

All your work and peace is gone –

How could this overtake you!

Are you caught by lovely youth

By that beloved form,

By those eyes so good and true,

By that all-powerful force?

When I try to run away,

Collect myself and flee,

In a moment my path strays

Back to her you see.

By that magic thread, so

That cannot be untied,

The dear wanton girl, oh

She holds me fast: and I

Must lie within her magic spell

And live where she may go.

How great the change, I tell!

Love! Love! Let me go!

Something Bothering by Paul Rossener

Why do I get this feeling
   that you are
hiding something
   from me
     from everyone
     from anyone
around you
   beside you

   can you
trust me
   just this once

Don't mistake
   my intention
   my intense attention
on the manner
   you folded your arms
   you scratched your neck
   you pinched your ear

You have something

I want to hear
I'm just curious

oh!
I don't want to be rude
I don't want to intrude
usually I just keep my mouth shut
and let things unfold

behold

Something's
bothering you
I can see it in your
eyes
am I right?
am I squeezing you too tight?
excuse my prying
eyes

It's just

I want to help you
no, no, no
you're right

you don't need my help
    I am
sorry
    I should prolly
    go;
it's been nice
    talking to you
    being with you

do you
    have something
else to say?

Okay
    that is
fine

Meet me
    sometime
    when the
east wind has blown
    your fair-weather friends

    I will be here

"He stepped down, trying not to look long at her, as if she were the sun, yet he saw her, like the sun, even without looking."

Torn Asunder by Peta Maria Slaney

"You can trust me" he said.

"I will never leave you.

I will never hurt you.

I will adore and love you always.

You complete me. You fix me.

You make me feel as though I could take on the world.

You are the answer I have been looking for my entire life.

I never thought I'd find a girl like you. I never want to be without you. I need you. You solve my problems. You kiss it all better.

I will never betray you.

I will never hurt you."

He lied. He broke my heart and left me here, torn asunder, trying to fix myself and put back together all the pieces of my broken heart.

"You're strong. You'll get over it"

Section Two

Self & Soul

Regret by Charlotte Bronte

Long ago I wished to leave

The house where I was born;

Long ago I used to grieve,

My home seemed so forlorn.

In other years, its silent rooms

Were filled with haunting fears;

Now, their very memory comes

O'ercharged with tender tears.

Life and marriage I have known,

Things once deemed so bright;

Now, how utterly is flown

Every ray of light !

'Mid the unknown sea of life

I no blest isle have found;

At last, through all its wild wave's strife,

My bark is homeward bound.

Farewell, dark and rolling deep !

Farewell, foreign shore !

Open, in unclouded sweep,

Thou glorious realm before !

Yet, though I had safely pass'd

That weary, vexed main,

One loved voice, through surge and blast,

Could call me back again.

Though the soul's bright morning rose

O'er Paradise for me,

William ! even from Heaven's repose

I'd turn, invoked by thee !

Storm nor surge should e'er arrest

My soul, exulting then:

All my heaven was once thy breast,

Would it were mine again !

Body Image by Anita Traynor

I've always lived inside my head
And assumed my body would manage without me,
A receptacle to carry my thoughts around in.

If I had noticed it was there
Could I have run a marathon?
Could I have climbed Ben Nevis?

If I had taken more care
Would I have had another child?
Would I have been spared my cancer?

My life as random as my fears
Painted on the skew in abstract
Vibrantly coloured and too loud
For many to recognise as art.

Priceless.

From The Scarlet Letter by Nathaniel Hawthorne

"She had not known the weight until she felt the freedom."

Doing Magic by Julia McGuinness

Three stamps - strawberry, green, chocolate,

behind matching Italian nobles' heads

tilted under hats tall as dustbins.

I shuffled them on a tray, snooty faces up,

crowned them with a plastic cup,

swirled them dizzy, yelled 'Abracadabra! '

like the magician on the telly,

swept up my cup with a flourish.

The pink stamp *really* vanished once.

A grey-voiced newsman at a desk

read stories about *gorilla* warfare

and all the sweet, sticky people

held *in custardy*.

Then the Ajax Tornado zoomed

round a black-and-white room

and everything sparkled clean.

I begged Mum to buy one,

but she just smiled, watched

all summer at the kitchen window

as I played by the old tree-stump.

I jumped off it again and again,

flapped my arms, desperate to fly.

"I am not what happened to me, I am what I choose to become."

From Crime and Punishment by Fyodor Dostoevsky

"To go wrong in one's own way is better than to go right in someone else's."

73

What's the difference between

depression and wisdom

falling apart and into place

giving up and giving in?

From Anna Karenina by Leo Tolstoy

"If you look for perfection, you'll never be content."

Would I change anything? Would I prefer to have taken a different path?

I would not be the woman I am today.

I would not be as strong as I am today.

I would not use my voice as I do today.

I would not have the fire that I have today.

I have seen pain, I have felt loss.

I have seen joy, I have known contentment.

Everything has happened has made me who I am and placed me here.

From the ashes of despair and loneliness,

To the high skies of love and confidence,

I rise up on the wings of eagles.

I am the Phoenix.

I am well again.

I am me.

"I am the wisest man alive, for I know one thing, and that
is that I know nothing."

From Crime and Punishment by Fyodor Dostoevsky

"It takes something more than intelligence to act intelligently."

From The Divine Comedy by Dante Alighieri

"The man who lies asleep will never waken fame, and his desire and all his life drift past him like a dream, and the traces of his memory fade from time like smoke in air, or ripples on a stream."

From Jane Eyre by Charlotte Bronte

"Do you think, because I am poor, obscure, plain and little, I am soulless and heartless? You think wrong! - I have as much soul as you, - and full as much heart! And if God had gifted me with some beauty and much wealth, I should have made it as hard for you to leave me, as it is now for me to leave you!"

Up by Paul Rossener

When I was a kid

I would always look at the sky

Hi

I would say to the bunny sitting next to the swan

My mom would ask

What do you see now

Wow

That is indeed a bunny right next to a swan

When I was a kid

I would always stare at the night

Right

I found the tail of the scorpion

My mom would ask

What is it honey

Golly

That looks like a tail of a scorpion

When I was a kid

I would always take a peek

Eek

I saw the witch on the moon again

My mom would ask

What's wrong my dear

Oh dear

There's a witch at the moon again

When I was a kid

My mom would ask

Above

What do you see my love

I would point my fingers

As my imagination lingers

Ma

Those two clouds right there

One's a mama and another's a baby bear

"We can know only that we know nothing. And that is the highest degree of human wisdom."

Just Try Me by Kaisa Hammaren-Ojanen

I see you are trying to approach me.

Before you proceed

please let me know

your armory and body count.

From Fanshawe by Nathaniel Hawthorne

"A single dream is more powerful than a thousand realities."

From Crime and Punishment by Fyodor Dostoevsky

"We sometimes encounter people, even perfect strangers, who begin to interest us at first sight, somehow suddenly, all at once, before a word has been spoken."

By C.G. Jung

"Loneliness does not come from having no people about
one, but from being unable to communicate the things
that seem important to oneself, or from holding certain
views which others find inadmissible."

The Future Path by Peta Maria Slaney

I'm not sure how I feel about the future,

The path seems to veer before me,

Turning this way and that,

Like a meandering river breaking off into subsidiaries.

Or perhaps it is more like a web,

The criss-cross of roads not taken and the possible
permutations of circumstance.

How will it end? Will I find happiness? Am I destined to
be alone or will I find the other half of my lost soul?

Does it matter anyway, if I am unhappy? One miserable
creature on this beautiful planet. Does it matter if my
stars do not align and my universe does not sing?

There is a choice. A choice before each one of us. A
choice to either loiter through our lives feeling unfulfilled
and angry at fate, or to open our hearts to the moment
and embrace what life brings to us.

I face the rising sun and stride towards the future.

Hope by Emily Dickinson

Hope is the thing with feathers -

That perches in the soul -

And sings the tune without the words -

And never stops - at all -

And sweetest - in the Gale - is heard -

And sore must be the storm -

That could abash the little Bird

That kept so many warm -

I've heard it in the chillest land -

And on the strangest Sea -

Yet - never - in Extremity,

It asked a crumb - of me.

Autumn Fog by Anita Traynor

I look down

There are feet kicking golden leaves.

I look round

There is a wisp of breath

A dog

Some trees

Sky.

I scream out

'Here I am'

And wait for someone to

Join up my dots and

Colour me in.

I wake

I yawn

I do stuff

I yawn

I sleep

I don't sleep

I breathe

I yawn.

Outside is the Autumn fog

Inside it is already and always winter.

I look down
There are hands
One holds a pen
It writes: enough.

"There is in every one of us, even those who seem to be most moderate, a type of desire that is terrible, wild, and lawless."

From The Blithedale Romance by Nathaniel Hawthorne

"No summer ever came back, and no two summers ever were alike. Times change, and people change; and if our hearts do not change as readily, so much the worse for us."

Presence by Paul Rossener

It's the third

time

today

that my mind

goes to rewind

yesterday

five years ago

my seventeenth birthday

then it runs forward

tomorrow

next month

my wedding day

I try to hold

my breath

for ten seconds

ten minutes

but it swings

back again

to the past
to what's next

to whenever

so like a fish
in a pond
I set
it free

swim
splash
saturate
yourself

but don't
go over
the pond
beyond

because

where you

live

is right here

right now

this second

this moment

at present

be present

From Inferno by Dante Alighieri

"Do not be afraid; our fate

Cannot be taken from us; it is a gift."

Snort,

turn your back

at me

once more and

I'll do nothing about it.

From The Brothers Karamazov by Fyodor Dostoevsky

"Above all, don't lie to yourself. The man who lies to himself and listens to his own lie comes to a point that he cannot distinguish the truth within him, or around him, and so loses all respect for himself and for others. And having no respect he ceases to love."

Solitary by Peta Maria Slaney

Solitary, like the moon.

Alone, but not without purpose.

Encased in a glass prison of my own design.

It is safer to be alone.

To be an Ice Queen.

An Empress of Solitude.

I feel as much as you.

I love as well as you.

I hurt as deeply as you.

But you will never know.

I will not tell you.

I shall not let you in.

You shall not break my protective cage of ice.

You will never know me.

From The Scarlet Letter by Nathaniel Hawthorne

"We dream in our waking moments, and walk in our sleep."

By C.G. Jung

"Knowing your own darkness is the best method for dealing with the darknesses of other people."

Describing with words

is doomed to fail.

Everything remarkable

is beyond reasoning, and

impossible to represent:

to be

experienced by oneself.

Depression by Peta Maria Slaney

I see, but I do not feel.

I hear, but words can not touch me.

I am invincible, for surely feeling nothing is better than

feeling sorrow.

The anaesthesia of my mind frees me from mental

drudgery.

And yet, is it not tragic,

That to protect itself, my mind

Has chosen not to feel

And instead I am shut off.

I watch as people go about

Their daily lives. Jealous of

Their easy emotion.

Still terrified of letting the Feelings in.

For surely

Before Happiness Must come Heartbreak

From The Scarlet Letter by Nathaniel Hawthorne

"No man, for any considerable period, can wear one face to himself and another to the multitude, without finally getting bewildered as to which may be the true."

"O human race, born to fly upward, wherefore at a little wind dost thou so fall?"

This Adulting Thing by Kaisa Hammaren-Ojanen

You

get worried when you don't remember the causes for

short term memory loss

binge eat toffee on your way to a yoga class

when given free time for a couple of hours

you sleep.

But then,

in a sudden moment of clarity, you understand that

    you are the only saviour you have

    most important things aren't things

    you get only what you take

    silence sounds so good

    there's no middle of the road

    you need a spark to ignite

oh, what is this absence of anguish, I can see it all,

kind-of-almost-happiness…

and then you are back to your normal state.

You have a kebab roll for a lunch

a glass of wine to celebrate yet one more day at work

without dying

skip your dinner and

eat several Snickers in the cupboard hiding from kids and

husband

play Candy Crush Saga past your bedtime

because you can.

Just because you can.

For T by Anita Traynor

In her prison

She cannot move beyond her pain.

Here is frustration, anger,

A wilderness of bitter cold stark unwellness.

She clamours to tailgate her visitors

But her way is blocked.

She is trapped. She fumes.

In her sanctuary

She settles into her calm.

Here is peace, acceptance,

A cosy camp with cake and cocoa.

She waves her visitors off with smiles

Knowing the world awaits her.

She is patient. She rests.

From Crime and Punishment by Fyodor Dostoevsky

"Pain and suffering are always inevitable for a large intelligence and a deep heart. The really great men must, I think, have great sadness on earth."

By C.G. Jung

"The privilege of a lifetime is to become who you truly are."

From The Brothers Karamazov by Fyodor
Dostoevsky

"The mystery of human existence lies not in just staying
alive, but in finding something to live for."

Treatment For The Unruly Mind by Kaisa Hammaren

Imagination

obeys you better

when you let it run free every once in a while

From The Scarlet Letter by Nathaniel Hawthorne

"No man, for any considerable period, can wear one face to himself and another to the multitude, without finally getting bewildered as to which may be the true."

"Consider your origin. You were not formed to live like brutes but to follow virtue and knowledge."

Section 3

Life & Death

Early Flowering by Julia McGuinness

The blossom frothed upon the grainy bough –

A cherry tree cascading bloom on bloom

to fete us to our grand new home down south.

Pink petals danced the sky outside my room,

till flower-flakes, all flecked with rain, descended.

Trampled to mash, deserting dust-green leaves,

their dizzy glory days, like ours, soon ended.

Four seasons on. Redundancy. We moved.

We'd pass by our old home with angled necks

to spy the Porsche parked upon the drive.

An exile from the garden space out back,

each May I'd miss that shell-pink splash of life

and sit in pale remembrance of its splendour,

in a house boxed in and bullied by leylandii.

Five Ways of Looking at a House by Peta Maria Slaney

1.

It's just a house.

That's all.

2.

Bricks and mortar.

A good investment.

Something to barter,

A step on the ladder.

3.

A nest to raise our young.

It's not a house, it's a home.

Somewhere they can always

Come back to.

A place always open and warm.

4.

This house is a prison,

A life I didn't choose.

Shackles on my freedom.

A gilded cage,

My warden a wolf in sheep's clothing.

No way of escape.

5.

It's an eyesore.

It's an infringement of our privacy.

These new builds overshadowing our gardens.

We worked hard, we invested,

We raised our families.

Now we shuffle about in too-big mausoleums,

Testaments to a life well lived,

Soon to be sold for care home fees.

Tender Forms of Envy by Kaisa Hammaren-Ojanen

They are so in flames!

Strolling around hometown

in the middle of the night,

expressing themselves bravely in secrecy.

Graffiti painters.

You know

they must be young!

No middle-aged would bother to

go out

in the prime time of sleeping.

Baby by Julia McGuinness

Sharp as lemons, the farm dog's howl

wrings the dawn, slips its stave of cage bars

to wince the air over fields and woods.

Past indifferent birdsong, buzz of early white van,

electric shaver, the kettle's whistle,

till it pierces my guest-room window up the hill.

My gut tautens at a cry of the comfortless:

A flow-tide of yelps oceans the anaglypta

with news images of dinghies, rippling with bodies:

Infants wail; elders keep silence.

The exiled dog howls on through breakfast.

My host shrugs. *I know, but what can you do?*

Borders must hold, decent distance kept

lest storms upend our worlds.

Later, the farmer's daughter walks the dog.

He muds his nose in earth; opens jaws

to devour air; lunges on his lead as I pass.

She chokes him back tight by her body,

smiles through neat teeth. *He's just a baby.*

I say *I know, I know.*

Firstborn by Peta Maria Slaney

They passed me the small, pink mass.

And laid him across my breast.

I looked into his eyes, held his tiny hand.

Delicate fingernails like paper-thin sea shells.

A little, warm soft body,

Smelling of happiness, nourishment and new beginnings.

I look into his eyes, and I know,

This is the soul of my soul.

I am home. He is my own.

One Of Those Days by Anita Traynor

Don't you just hate it when
The tap runs hot onto your toothbrush and
You completely forget that you've just washed your face
with a steamy flannel and
Instead of a minty zing your mouth gets a soggy warm
rush of acrid bristles

And all because
You dreamed.
It took so long to find a place to be alone together
You opened door after door, each room full. Until
A breeze blew in and took you both out to sea

Awaking still searching confused groggy disappointed.
Sad. Salty sea taste.

You burn the toast and the milk's off and

The traffic's appalling

The sunshine is harsh

 This day is another soul assault

You planted forget-me-nots when he died

Quite unnecessary.

From Crime and Punishment by Fyodor Dostoevsky

"The darker the night, the brighter the stars,

The deeper the grief, the closer is God!"

The Big C by Peta Maria Slaney

"I've got cancer"

Her voice was the same

But the words were so wrong.

It was the voice I'd heard in my childhood.

The same reassuring tone.

"It's all going to be ok.

Everything will be fine."

The complete confidence

Of someone who knows

Their time is up and

They have made their peace with it.

She mustn't die

Don't leave me

Please don't go Mum.

Life by Charlotte Bronte

Life, I believe, is not a dream

So dark as sages say;

Oft a little morning rain

Foretells a pleasant day.

Sometimes there are clouds of gloom,

But these are transient all;

If the shower will make the roses bloom,

O why lament its fall ?

Rapidly, merrily,

Life's sunny hours flit by,

Gratefully, cheerily,

Enjoy them as they fly !

What though Death at times steps in

And calls our Best away ?

What though sorrow seems to win,

O'er hope, a heavy sway ?

Yet hope again elastic springs,

Unconquered, though she fell;

Still buoyant are her golden wings,

Still strong to bear us well.

Manfully, fearlessly,

The day of trial bear,

For gloriously, victoriously,

Can courage quell despair !

For Tia by Julia McGuinness

One day I will open my kitchen window, no longer watching

for you to appear on the sill in a magician's flourish,

staging your entrance with a meow for a second breakfast.

Your sunny spot on the sofa will be imprinted with a smile.

I will wake in the hour before dawn, with clear eyes

in the purrless silence of the dark, remembering yours,

how they gleamed green as gems as our gaze linked worlds;

how you explored each day as if it was your first. Or last.

And I will look again across the Whitby Road,

to the flower-bed where I hoped I'd found you asleep,

mistaking the breeze that rippled your black fur for breath

till outstretched fingers stroked the cold, hard truth.

Someday, Yesterday will flick her tail high in greeting,

settle herself to warm my body with a lapful of memories.

No more tears then. But today it only hurts.

"For to fear death, my friends, is only to think ourselves wise without really being wise, for it is to think that we know what we do not know. For no one knows whether death may not be the greatest good that can happen to man."

October by Kaisa Hammaren-Ojanen

In the garden

a parade of pouting flowers

A view from the bus window

is a wet grayscale drawing

A man sits on the stairs of a champagne bar

drinks beer from a can

The backpack gang gabbles at the traffic lights

Pieces of death

every day

She didn't open her eyes anymore

nurse opened the window

for the soul to fly out.

From The Divine Comedy by Dante Alighieri

"Through me you pass into the city of woe:

Through me you pass into eternal pain:

Through me among the people lost for aye.

Justice the founder of my fabric moved:

To rear me was the task of power divine,

Supremest wisdom, and primeval love.

Before me things create were none, save things

Eternal, and eternal I shall endure.

All hope abandon, ye who enter here."

Westminster 22/03/2017 by Anita Traynor

Mummy where are you?

Mummy why didn't you pick us up from school today?

It wasn't snowy, you weren't ill this morning.

You didn't tell us someone else was coming.

Mummy I'm scared. Mummy I'm frightened. Mummy I
don't understand.

People keep telling me nasty stories. They say you've gone
away.
They say you're not coming back.

But we know you wouldn't do that. You're our mummy.
You love us.
You wouldn't leave us.

Mummy please, I want a hug. Please stop this now, and come home.

I don't like this. I don't like not knowing where you are.

I don't like you not being here. I don't understand.

Mummy where are you? Mummy where are you?

Because I Could Not Stop For Death by Emily Dickinson

Because I could not stop for Death

He kindly stopped for me

The Carriage held but just Ourselves

And Immortality.

We slowly drove – He knew no haste

And I had put away

My labor and my leisure too,

For His Civility

We passed the School, where Children strove

At Recess in the Ring

We passed the Fields of Gazing Grain

We passed the Setting Sun

Or rather He passed Us

The Dews drew quivering and Chill

For only Gossamer, my Gown

My Tippet – only Tulle

We paused before a House that seemed

A Swelling of the Ground

The Roof was scarcely visible

The Cornice in the Ground

Since then 'tis Centuries and yet

Feels shorter than the Day

I first surmised the Horses' Heads

Were toward Eternity

Ship Gate *from Chester City Walls* by Julia McGuinness

The hole in the Wall was not cast aside

but borne, piece by piece, to the Park,

a stone's throw away, and re-assembled

as breath held across a path.

Its grainy sandstone frame, braced

against weight of sky, rainbows

an open space that lacks the gate

to separate ship from city.

Scabbed over with slabs, the Wall

is unsettled as all torn places

when mended. Gaps, transplanted

to discreet glades, lace through lives.

They seep memories, mapped by scars,

wince under strangers' stumblings,

are anointed by their listenings. Spaces

honoured, enfleshed alike by sun and rain.

Death by Peta Maria Slaney

The icy lump of loss sits in the pit of my stomach,

A constant reminder that you are no longer here.

I carry the burden of this loss.

It touches everything that I do and all that I feel.

Never again will you hold me in your arms,

Never again will I fold myself into you.

My rock, my centre has gone.

I say your name aloud and it dances in the air before me,

Shimmering and flickering as it fades away.

It fades away like a whisper,

An echo of a past love.

Our shared memories, our inside jokes, the unspoken and

Undoubted bond between us is now felt only by me.

It exists only in my mind and heart and I need to tell

Myself that it was real.

It was tangible.

I drag myself up and try to stumble through my life with
only half a heart.

A heart that can no longer leap as high, and has touched
the very depths of sorrow.

The light in your eyes

The exact curve of your lips

The lines on your face

The feel of your skin.

I try to imprint them in my mind, to memorize them,

To fight the forgetting as you fade away.

On The Death of Anne Bronte by Charlotte Bronte

There's little joy in life for me,

And little terror in the grave ;

I 've lived the parting hour to see

Of one I would have died to save.

Calmly to watch the failing breath,

Wishing each sigh might be the last ;

Longing to see the shade of death

O'er those belovèd features cast.

The cloud, the stillness that must part

The darling of my life from me ;

And then to thank God from my heart,

To thank Him well and fervently ;

Although I knew that we had lost

The hope and glory of our life ;

And now, benighted, tempest-tossed,

Must bear alone the weary strife.

Acknowledgments & Copyright Permissions

Contributors to the INFJ Anthology

Anita Traynor

Anita is 57 years old and lives in Suffolk with her partner Geoff. They are both introverts and enjoy staying at home, but they do love their sports cars and if you are lucky you may get a rare sighting of them out and about on the county's quiet back roads in the summer time.

Their children Dan and Bill are grown up and leading very exciting lives out in the big wide world. Anita travels the globe in their pockets while she spends her time pottering and noodling. She loves to walk with her best friend, boxer dog Ruby, and she likes to write, bake, read, sing, meditate, be mindful and practice yoga.

Having worked for too many years in a role that clashed with her INFJness, Anita decided to leave and re-train as a counsellor. A breast cancer diagnosis and the death of her mother led her to re-prioritise and now she's decided not to get back on the treadmill. This means she can't afford to go far or do much. Perfect! So she volunteers at a local community cafe, and she is an ambassador for an on-line cancer support group, working mostly from her armchair.

Peta Maria Slaney

Peta Maria Slaney is a writer and poet who lives in London with her husband and two children. She has always had a passion for literature, especially poetry. An anthology of her poems was published in spring 2017, as well as various articles and fiction pieces that have been published online.

She is also fascinated with psychology and enjoys study of the Myers-Briggs Personality Type Indicator. She has sought to combine her passions in this book.

You can find Peta Maria at her website :

www.astarthatdanced.wordpress.com

Or follow her on Twitter @astarthatdanced; and Facebook @petamariaslaney

Julia McGuinness

Julia McGuinness is a writer, counsellor and workshop facilitator. She is also a Registered Myers-Briggs Practitioner. As Creative Connections Cheshire, she brings these together, expressing the particular INFJ penchant for making fresh links. She runs writing workshops for well-being and belongs to the Lapidus network of therapeutic writing practitioners. She has also devised and run a workshop on Myers-Briggs type and writing style: Who We Are is How We Write.

Julia's poems have been anthologised and published online. Her first poetry collection, Chester City Walls, was published by Poetry Space in 2015. She has written four books including Growing Spiritually with the Myers-Briggs Model and Writing our Faith - both with SPCK.

Julia's study, like her mind, kaleidoscopes into chaos in the midst of creative projects. Afterwards, she feels compelled to tidy up and restore some sort of external order. Since the bookshelves are full, her cupboards are home to all the journals and poems she has written down the years to help her track her way through life.

Acknowledgements for her poems included here are due to Clear Poetry, Poetry Space, Chester Poets, Silver Birch Press, Spilling Cocoa Over Martin Amis and Ink, Sweat and Tears.

You can find Julia at www.creativeconnectionscheshire.co.uk or follow her on @CreatConneChesh

Kaisa Hammaren-Ojanen

Kaisa Hammaren-Ojanen is a Finnish writer. Love for words has got her into literature studies and she's working on her masters thesis on recovery narrative in a rock n' roll autobiography.

When she's not studying, writing, or selling paint and flowers in the supermarket, she's at home with her family, usually reading or napping. She loves cats, nature, travelling and snorkelling.

Paul Rossener

Paul Rossener Regonia is a Filipino teacher by profession and by heart. Most of the times, he can be found in the classroom, teaching artificial intelligence to undergraduate students. Some other times, he's in the lab, fiddling with a brain scanning device. But when out of sight, he is probably reading Lemony Snicket, capturing a snapshot for the day, or having his quiet time.

Paul has composed numerous pieces, albeit unpublished ones. He has written autobiographies, short fictions, song lyrics (but without tune -- he has his limits too); as well as speeches, lectures, and sermons. At the moment, his most favorite is his romantic confessional series, disclosed only to a small group of friends. He dreams of publishing a children's book about superheroes and mental health.

Email: paulheartjesus@gmail.com

As mentioned in the preface, these are all authors who have been identified as INFJs posthumously by members of the Myers-Briggs community. Their writing style and subjects give a good indication as to their personality type and temperament. As they all passed away before 1947, their works are in the public domain.

Charlotte Bronte

1816-1855. She was an English novelist and poet. Her works include Jane Eyre and Villette.

Fyodor Dostoevsky

1821-1888. Dostoevsky was a Russian novelist, short story writer, essayist, journalist and philosopher. He is known for The Brothers Karamazov, The Idiot, and Crime and Punishment.

C.G. Jung

1875-1961. Carl Jung was a Swiss psychoanalyst and psychiatrist. His analysis of psychological types led to the development of the Myers-Briggs Type Indicator.

Plato

428-348BC. Plato was a Greek philosopher and he established the first institute of higher learning; The Academy in Athens. His theories form the basis for many western political philosophies.

Goethe

1749-1832. Johann Wolfgang von Goethe was a German writer, poet and critic.

His most famous drama is Faust and he was a literary celebrity by the age of 25.

Nathaniel Hawthorne

1804-1864. Hawthorne was an American writer famous for his short stories and novels. His works include Fanshawe and the Scarlet Letter.

Dante Alighieri

C.1265-1312. Dante's masterpiece The Divine Comedy has been referred to as the greatest work of the middle ages. In Italian, he is referred to as Il Sommo Poeta- the supreme poet.

Emily Bronte

1818-1848. Emily Bronte is sister to the aforementioned Charlotte Bronte. Her only novel is Wuthering Heights; a classic of English literature.

Leo Tolstoy

1828-1910. Count Lev Nikolayevich Tolstoy is best known for his works Anna Karenina, and War and Peace. He was born into an aristocratic Russian family and is widely regarded as one of the greatest authors of all time.

Emily Dickinson

1830-1886. Emily Dickinson was an American poet. A complete collection of her poetry was first published in 1955; the sheer breadth of her work was not discovered until after she had passed away.

www.ingramcontent.com/pod-product-compliance
Lightning Source LLC
Chambersburg PA
CBHW070123260726
48658CB00001B/244